SINOSRAUM

CHINA'S EXPANSIONISM

IPSEETA BISWAL

Contents

Preface   v

  1. Lebensraum   1

  2. World War 1   6

  3. World War Ii   9

  4. Historical Background Of China's Land Grabbing 14

  5. Xinjiang And Its Subtle Incorporation   24

  6. Capture Of The Roof Of The World   30

  7. Two Pronged War With India   37

  8. North East Frontier Agency (nefa) Or Arunachal 45

    Pradesh

  9. South China Sea On Fire   51

10. Sikkim   57

11. Bhutan   61

12. Central Asian Borders   65

13. Taiwan   69

14. Belt And Road Initiative (bri)   77

15. Red Bully   83

16. Modern China   90

17. China's Lebensraum Strategy   94

18. How To Counter Sinosraum   101

References   107

Preface

The book encapsulates the shrewd strategy of China in expanding its territories and subsequently managing them in what is termed Sinosraum, while the rest of the world made some feeble noises.Beginning with the concept of Lebensraum which was at the heart of German expansionism in the World Wars, it dwells into the historical dynasties of China and how their territorial conquests have been made the basis for the communist regime to annex territories. The subtle conquest of Xinjiang, overunning of Tibet, a two front war with India and the classic nibbling strategy in the South China Sea have all been highlighted. it further goes on to look at the future gameplan of the regime as they look at consolidating their territories as also eye Taiwan. It also looks at how modern China has developed and is the envy of many, The book ends with a note on how the world should respond to this strategy of China.

CHAPTER ONE

Lebensraum

The term *"Lebensraum"* translated as *"Living Space"* was made famous by Friedrich Ratzel, a German ethnographer and geographer in his book Politische Geographie. It has been defined as a geographical space area required to support a living species at its current population size and mode of existence.

However, it was first used by Oscar Peschel in the review of Charles Darwin book, *"The Origin of Species"* in 1860. This term was loosely translated as the need for physical space for settlement of people. Johann Rudolf Kjellen, a Swedish political scientist further expounded on the theory of Ratzel.

We begin with Oscar Peschel who wrote a review of Darwin's *"On the Origin of Species by Means of Natural Selection"* in the journal *"Las Ausland"* of which he was the editor. He developed the term *"Lebensraum"* stating that origin and evolution of species is contingent on the geographical landscape or morphology.

Ratzel is his book *"Political Geography"*, drew similarities between a nation state and living organism in their struggle for space, which also resulted in conflict. Another interesting similarity that he expounded was that akin to differentiated functions of the body controlled by a central organ, a state also had to expand through a spatial division of labour. Lebensraum was described by him as a synthetic concept of biological, geographical and anthropological conditions which led to the desire for space. Inspired by Moritz Wagner's, *"Migration Theory"*, he stated that continuous geographical expansion was a sine quo non for the rise of great powers and vitality of the State. His concept of planetary space was that given the finite space in our planet, this expansionism leads to the final structure of only a few large nations. Ratzel, went onto expand the Darwinian concept of *"struggle for existence"* as actually a struggle for space. Further, in his view, the size of the nation is dependent on both the growth of its population and its metabolic needs. On racial aspects, he mentioned that the strength of a nation is in its blending of races such as in the British Isles.

Rudolf Kjellen's explanation of Lebensraum was on the basis of integrating two aspects of State policy namely its ethnopolitics and its geopolitics. He coined the terms *"geopolitik"*, *"ecopolitik"* and *"demopolitik"*, all critical elements of Lebensraum. Thus in his view, the geographical position, economic factor and demographic profile influence a State's outlook on expansionism. Like Ratzel, he did recognize the power of racially diverse population in building the strength of a nation. His concept was based on a State becoming an organic territory by seeking geographic individuals to which it can connect and thereby deepen natural territory. The concept of geographic individuals is manifested by a dual movement i.e. outwards towards its natural boundaries and inwards harmoniously towards its natural territory. It's about the State reshaping its land so as to live up to its increased demands by developing its pre-dispositions and overcoming its shortcomings. This in effect makes the land more natural than it originally was thereby increasing the efficiency of its utilization and ensuring it can sustain higher populations. Kjellen's theory of Lebensraum does not seek territorial expansion unlike that of Ratzel.

Subsequently Karl Haushofer also jumped into the fray with his publication *"Zeitschrift fur Geopolitik"* which dwelt on the operationalization of Lebensraum. One of his pupils was the famous Rudolf Hess, the right hand man of Adolf Hitler. It was here that Hausofer got sucked into the realpolitik of the Reich and was instrumental in the conceptualization of *"Mein Kampf"* when the Fuhrer was incarcerated at Landsberg Fortress prison. Even the plan for the Nazi regimes eastern front conquests manifested in the *"Generalplan Ost"* which emanated from the work of Haushofer.

As indicated earlier, the real ground level implementation of this term emanated during the World Wars and was used chiefly by the World War 1 Axis Powers namely Germany, Italy and Japan to further their territorial ambitions. However, the Nazis used it to their advantage to rabble rouse the Germans for avenging what they called was the humiliation of the country in World War 1. It thus remains a loathed term in geopolitics but the blame for this cannot solely lie at the feet of these famous geographers and political scientists. The political pundits of the Axis regime and the Nazis clearly twisted these theories to suit their objective of territorial expansion. This book seeks to look at how the Chinese, learning from the world wars, have re-moulded Lebensraum, to suit their nefarious objective of land grabbing to expand their empire. This could well be christened as Sinosraum.

• 5 •

CHAPTER TWO

World War 1

When the war triggered by the assassination of Archduke Ferdinand began in 1914; the concept of Lebensraum had not seeped in deep into the thought process of military strategists. However, during the course of the war, a situation developed wherein the Allies created a naval blockade of the Axis Powers based in central Europe. This led to severe shortages, especially of agricultural products and natural resources for the manufacturing sector. Even the supplies from the African colonies of the Axis Powers could not breach this blockade, thereby creating an economically precarious situation.

As a result of this blockade, clarion calls for Lebensraum thus emanated within Germany. The concept was premised on the fact that one needed to occupy territories to ensure supplies in case of emergencies like this war. The protagonists alluded to Eastern Europe and

Russia being sources of agricultural and mineral resources while the African colonies could also supply many raw materials.

The fructification of this plan took place in September 1914 at the beginning of the World War and is named as the "*Septemberprogramm*". Formulated by the Chancellor's private secretary Kurt Riezler, the plan looked at annexation of Belgium, Luxembourg, parts of France and the Russian empire. The plan, relatively more modest than the subsequent Nazi plan was to expand both eastwards and westwards as well into the African colonies of the other powers. However, the plan ran into rough weather as the Germans could not overrun France and were engaged in a long battle of attrition marked by trench warfare. Ultimately, they were defeated and all the subsequent grandiose expansionism was nipped in the bud.

However, the plan when dissected in detail, apart from the territories annexed, had many subtle elements to it. Firstly, the whole plan with expansionism at the core of it was to have a counterweight to the British Empire without directly waging a battle with it. It was this thinking that emanated in the concept of "*Mitteleuropa*" in the mainland. Even in the Africa expansion known as "*Mittelafrika*", emphasis was laid on capturing the Belgian and French colonies so that the German conquests could compare with the British colonies in Africa. Secondly, importance was laid on access to raw materials which was crucial to development of the pan German empire. The iron ore mines in France and the resources in Africa were part of this plan. The territorial expansion into the Russian empire would also satiate this need. Thirdly, buffer states such as Poland and Finland were to be created between it and the Russian empire with a view to ensuring political stability.

While the Germans were effectively neutralized in the western front, they did manage to eke out some territorial concessions from Russia and Romania on the eastern front. Nevertheless, at the end of the war they were on the losing end and all their nefarious designs came to nought.

CHAPTER THREE

World War II

The interwar period saw a lot of disenchantment within Germany in what was perceived to be a lopsided Versailles Treaty that had enervated the once strong nation and made them lose territory. The German nationalists jumped into the fray eager to leverage this seething anger and propagated Lebensraum. The Ratzelanian concept was of a nation adapting successfully to one geographic territory and then logically expanding. The nation state was compared with an organism that needed space to expand. The overpopulation was cited as a reason for Germany seeking more territory to which migration was needed.

The Nazis were the most effective geopolitical users of Lebensraum as they took cue from Karl Haushofer's school. It was centred around avenging the humiliation of World War 1 and the Treaty of Versailles. The three pronged rationale as also expounded in Hitler's Mein Kampf were the need to restore lost pride, overpopulation needing to be settled and provision of natural resources. They also propagated the racial superiority of the Germanic people over the slavics in Eastern Europe namely Ukraine, Poland and Russia. The entire war was sold to the German people on this theory. This deadly concoction is what brainwashed the population and the Nazis started their operations eastwards attacking Czechoslovakia.

Ironically, Hitler in his autobiography had also painted a positive picture of the American westward expansion which had led to the genocide of the native Red Indians. The dependency on food imports during World War 1 was used as a pretext for territorial expansion and capture of areas in Eastern Europe which could then act as food bowls for the Germans.

This theory was further propounded by Hitler in his second book where he sought to conquer new territories for the Germans. The aim was to establish the Great German Reich which would rule over a thousand years. The target for Lebensraum was Russia since it provided the agricultural land and natural resources for the German state. The aim was also to keep the German bloodline pure and purge it off the other nationalities. The pernicious thought process of the Nazis stretched Lebensraum beyond what the proponents ever thought of. It was tantamount to ethnic cleansing of many of the communities of non-Germanic origin, chiefly the Jews. Strangely, the Nazis also differentiated between different strands of non-Germans. For them, those in Western Europe and Scandinavia could still co-exist with Germans but the rest of the territories that they intended to occupy were placed on a different pedestal with a view to being discriminated in all walks of life.

Thus the concept of Lebensraum was stretched to limits which even its originators could never have remotely conceived. More than territorial expansion, it was about racial profiling and genocide which in the Germans view would lead to continuation of a superior race.

The Nazis were quite successful in implementing Lebensraum in the first couple of years of the war. Their tank formation known as the Panzers and the air force called the Luftwaffe managed to steamroll along the mainland capturing France and reaching to the outskirts of the major Soviet cities like Leningrad, Moscow and Stalingrad. However, defeat by the Soviet forces at all the three cities turned the tide of the war from which they could never recover. The fall of Berlin ended their infamy in 1945.

Some may argue that the Chinese policies in Xinjiang are not far from what the Nazis believed in. The only difference is that the latter is being done subtly without the leadership tom-toming about it. Moreover, there are no overt statements from the leadership that suggests that the Hans are a superior race to the original inhabitants of the provinces that the Chinese have annexed. Nevertheless, deep down the Politburo believes in this racial superiority doctrine which has necessitated the large scale settlement of Hans in these provinces. It would firstly completely alter the demographic profile of the region and could facilitate the authorities in clamping down. While one may argue that the infamous concentration camps don't exist, but the indoctrination camps are not far off. Moreover, with the advances in medical science, it may not be incorrect to speculate that the Chinese may be using scientific techniques for mind control rather than having to resort to torture techniques like the gas chambers of yore. As for the genocide of communities, while the Chinese have not directly targeted anyone unlike the Nazis, they have focused on vulnerable sections like women. This ploy was used in both Tibet and Xinjiang to create a sense of fear.

As for the military strategy of the 2nd World War, the Chinese may have learnt from the mistakes of the Reich. The blatant aggression was only seen in the case of Tibet where the forces literally exploited an opportunity of global indecision to capture the entire territory. Even the US intervention was lukewarm while the rest of the world just made some feeble noises as Lhasa fell in a jiffy and the Dalai Lama had to take refuge in India. Even India was not in a position to interfere and tried to maintain cordial relations with the communist party.

Xinjiang was usurped smartly as the Chinese teamed up with the Russians who were more interested in ensuring peace in the Central Asian Republics which was part of the Soviet Union. The war with India on two fronts was also an opportune time as both Russia and US were busy with the Cuban missile crisis. For the rest of the territories, the Chinese have increased their military might and have been using the nibbling strategy to unsettle their adversaries.

CHAPTER FOUR

Historical background of China's land grabbing

Chinese thought process on expansionism could be traced to the mandarin name of the country itself. China is known as Zhongguo, whereby Zhong translates into *"the centre of the world"* and Guo is *"country"*. Thus Chong Quo would literally mean that it is a country at the centre of the world or is the Middle Kingdom. This may well interpreted as the centrality of China in global affairs. This has been stretched by its policy makers of late to subtly look at domination over the other cultures. This is an indirect reference to both the geo-centricity of the country and the fact that global growth has to take place around it.

A related aspect to this is the concept of Han chauvinism, including that of the *"Great Han"* has been propounded. It is also believed that the Han people are at the centre of mankind. This has been the basis on which the concept of expansionism including through the settlement of the Han people in the annexed territories has been propagated.

Before, we get into how China implemented its Lebensraum, let us look at why China suddenly resorted to this territorial expansionism after independence. Chinese civilisations have always propagated this idea and engaged in wars with neighbours to assert their influence and dominance. The frontiers of the Kingdom have always been the subject of intense interest both with a view to send a chilling message to any misadventure that might be attempted as also the need to expand.

The Qin dynast, laid the edifice of this principle as it united the Han kingdoms into the region. It also made contact with the ancient Yue tribes and original denizens of the Korean peninsula. Subsequently, the Han dynasty conquered North Korea and North Vietnam while also making foray into some parts of modern Xinjiang. After a hiatus due to the population loss and the need for consolidation, the Sui dynasty then attempted to conquer Korea but its campaign was cut short. The Tang dynasty went into its expansionist mode recapturing

Korea and North Vietnam while making forays into Xinjiang and Tibet. However, it vacated the latter. With the collapse of the Tang dynasty, most of its acquisitions including Vietnam became independent. In the 13th century, the Yuan dynasty then went into an expansionist spree even invading the Pagan kingdom in modern Myanmar. It had successes in Korea and Tibet.

However, it was in the 17th century when the Qing dynasty established the largest sphere of influence of the Chinese kingdoms. The Qings were ironically Manchus from the Manchuria region who united through large grouping called banners. However, they also assimilated the Han Chinese into their administrative structures. They conquered the frontiers, piggybacking on the strong cavalry and artillery. This neutralised the advantages of the nomadic horsemen, such as those of the Dzunghar Khanate in the Central Asian Steppes. One of the largest historical genocides, estimated to be over a million,that of the Dzunghars, was undertaken during this period by this dynasty.

The Qings made successful forays into Mongolia, Tibet and Xinjiang. They attacked Korea and some of the regions in modern Kazakhstan, Kyrgyzstan and Tajikistan. They even managed to invade Taiwan and capture the island. The territorial expansion went to the extent of them even claiming the island of Sakhalin.

The Qings however had to taste defeat in Myanmar during 1765-1769. However, despite this, they harboured ambitions of making it part of their territory. After the collapse of the Qing dynasty in 1911, the Republic of China took over the reins. However, both outer Mongolia and Tibet declared their independence but were not recognised by the former.

It was a period of consolidation but external influences such as that of the Japanese empire was felt. The collapse of the Qings also led to the vacuum in power that was exploited by both Japan and the Soviet Union. The Japanese tried to control some key parts of China through the 21 point demand made during 1915 at the time of World War 1. They also attacked Manchuria in 1931 in a guise of a staged incident. The Soviets fought a battle for control of the China Eastern Railway which led to them defeating the army of the Republic in 1929.

However, World War II changed the dynamics with the Republic trying to assert its influence in Korea and South East Asia. A foray was also made into North Vietnam but the Chinese civil war saw the overthrow of the Republic and takeover by the communist People's Republic. This was the turning point for expansionism as the Communists poked their nose and engaged to expand across all territories. They also smartly used the window of opportunity in this period when all the colonial powers were licking their wounds after the devastating economic effect of World War II.

The conquest of Xinjiang was undertaken with ease including with the support from the Soviets. Forays were made into Tibet as they nibbled territories coming to the doorstep of Lhasa. Eventually, the Dalai Lama was forced to flee to India and the territory was annexed. North Vietnam was another theatre where the People's Republic ventured by supporting North Vietnam. This war lasted two decades with the victory of the North Vietnamese forces in 1975. The Chinese could thus not implement their Lebensraum here since there were too many players in the fray after the defeat of the US. Nevertheless, the installation of a communist government in the country was the next best option to which the Chinese had to reconcile with.

The Korean war was however, an opportunity for them to showcase their military prowess. With the colonial powers decimated by the war, US was the only real powerhouse at that time and even they were given a tough fight. While the latter managed to save South Korea, they were pushed back from the North Korean territory by the Chinese who even managed to take Seoul a few times. The battle of the Chosin Reservoir, made famous by a movie, showed their prowess in multi-pronged and flanking attacks on even the mighty US ground forces. While they suffered heavy casualties in that, they were able to chase off the strong Americans from North Korea. This would surely have given them lots of confidence to complete the other territorial conquests such as Tibet.

Communist China subsequently waged a war against India in 1962 and captured the region of Aksai Chin in Ladakh. They also took over Arunachal Pradesh which they argued was part of South Tibet but retreated. China again asserted in 1967 its claim over Sikkim which was then an Indian protectorate. There were two skirmishes at Nathu La and Cho La during September-October, 1967. While the versions are different, as in any such incident, India managed to hold onto its position and the Sikkim-Tibet border got effectively resolved after this. Sikkim eventually integrated into

India in 1975.

Subsequently in 1974, China also engaged in a battle for the Paracel Islands with Vietnam. They managed to inflict heavy damage on the South Vietnamese navy and capture these islands. It was possibly the first full scale sea battle that the Chinese were engaged in and for the first time showed the prowess of their naval forces. The salami slicing technique used in the Spratly Islands in a multi country dispute exposed their classic re-adaptation of the Lebensraum by brute show of force.

China has been historically applying the principle of Lebensraum in its own subtle way trying to chip away and usurp territory of kingdoms around it. While not openly propagating it, the strategy has been to wage battles, use the classic colonial principle of divide and rule and change the demographics of the region by settlement of Chinese from elsewhere. The latter has been supplemented with the security mechanism provided to these settlers.

Another smart tactic used by them has been to use any world crisis as an appropriate entry point. The rest of the world would then be embroiled in the crisis and they could subtly achieved their territorial ambitions without any resistance. Some of the classic cases are that of Tibet when the 1950s says little appetite from the World War adversaries to engage meaningfully. Moreover, US was also embroiled in the Korean war which was an opportune time to enter in 1950. The two front war with India is another classic example when the Chinese used the Cuban missile crisis for an opportune time to enter and attack India. Even in the 2022 Ukraine crisis when the Russians have been trying to capture the former, they would surely be toying around with the idea of annexation of Taiwan as both the US and its NATO allies seek to defuse the crisis.

They have understood that security is one of the primary tools to ensure the success of this nibbling away strategy. Hence, even today wherever China seeks to make investment, especially in areas prone to law and order problems, they have taken their security apparatus with them and establish their own little self-contained fiefdoms.

Being the shrewd businessmen that they are, they have also put in place systems for ensuring an increased debt burden and then set in place a recovery mechanism. This classic tactic takes us back to our colonial days when the powers that be used the same mechanism to bleed the economy and usurp assets like land.

On the social front, the Chinese have used the tactics of intimidation to suppress the local resistance movements. This has been through dividing the resistance movements as well as perpetuating atrocities on the vulnerable sections like women. Taking a cue from the Qing dynasty's maltreatment of Ughyur women including raping them, the Chinese have continued to use the strategy in both Tibet and Xinjiang.

Moreover, they have, like the colonial powers created infrastructure in these regions primarily with a view to ensure easy access for their military forces, in case of any emergency situation. It has also facilitated settlements by attracting the Han Chinese to these regions. However, it is important to also give credit to the Chinese for having changed the entire connectivity of the regions they conquered, even in treacherous conditions and altitudes like Tibet. This has definitely given a fillip to the economy of these regions and improved their growth parameters, even if the same has not been equitous for the original denizens of those lands.

The Chinese have also used historical references of their dynasties to justify their Sinosraum. Chiefly, it has been the Yuan and Qing dynasties whose rule over these disputed regions which has been used as a rationale for China to usurp territories. What is significant to note that the Qing dynasty which has been the bedrock of the Chinese historian's explanation was founded by the Manchu bannermen who originate from Mongolia.

CHAPTER FIVE

Xinjiang and its subtle incorporation

The area that we now know as Xinjiang was ethically two separate regions right from its ancient history. It was geographically divided by the Tian Shan mountains. The northern part was known as the Dzungharia and the southern part as the Tarim Basin. Dzungaria was inhabited largely by the Mongol speaking Dzunghars with the southern part by Ugyhurs as well as the Turks. However, the history of these two regions indicates settlement by others groups as well.

Historically, the southern part was ruled in the 2nd century BC by the Xiongnu empire emerging from the nomadic denizens of modern Mongolia, followed by their defeat in around 60 BC to the Han dynasty which ruled till the 3rd century AD. The Hans made a series of expeditions into the Tarim Basin and managed to nibble away at the Xiongnu empire with the support of the Yuezhis. After a period of nearly 3 century rule by local Buddhist chiefs, the region fell into the hands of the Turks and subsequently, the Tang dynasty. The Tibetan empire also went on an expansion spree during this period and managed to defeat the Tangs for a brief period before the latter recovered their lost land. The Ugyhur's then came into power and ruled until the 9th century AD after which the Turks resurfaced and the region saw Islam as the predominant religion. In a see saw turn of events, the Tarim Basin fell into the hands of the Mongol Empire before the Turks won it back. A series of Turkish kingdoms or Khanates ruled over the region. Finally the Dzunghar's who ruled northern Xinjiang conquered the Tarim Basin around the 17th century. Their rule including the levy of taxes and spread of Buddhism led to some tension with the Ugyhur's.

Xinjiang came under the rule of the Qing dynasty in the 1750 and they ruled over it for more than 160 years until the latter's downfall in 1911. The rule began when the Dzunghar's lost to the Qing's and the region was made a province of China in 1884. The battles between the Dzunghar's and the Qing's was prolonged but the former were defeated and subjected to genocide with their population being virtually wiped out and some escaping to neighbouring regions. They also undertook a lot of atrocities on the Ugyhur's including raping their women.

However, it was the Qing dynasty that despite the cultural diversity of the two regions, strategized to integrate these into the unified Xinjiang province. It was in this period that the Qing dynasty encouraged the minorities in Xinjiang like the Uighurs as well as the Manchus and Hans to settle down in the region and change its demography. They believed that they were carrying forward the Han and Tang era and restoring the region under the Chinese rule. Moreover, they also introduced the concept of China being a multicultural society including its Muslim Ugyhurs.

With the collapse of the Qing dynasty in 1911, the Republic of China took over. However, there was a revolt against the Chinese rule from the erstwhile Dzunghars. There was also a move by the Mongols to unify themselves in the northern part. On the other hand, rebellions in the Tarim Basin led to the formation of the 1st East Turkistan Republic. However, this was suppressed by the Muslim Chinese warlord Ma Zhongying. The 2nd East Turkistan Republic with Soviet support was established in 1943 but with the Chinese revolution and the communists coming to power, they were forced to negotiate with the new regime and a sizeable number of their leaders were killed in a plane crash on the way to Beijing for negotiations.

Communist China immediately occupied Xinjiang in 1949 and the Turkistan Republic movement also petered out. The People's Republic of China (PRC) then pursued a policy of settlement of the Han and Hui Chinese in the Dzungharia region thereby altering the demographic profile. The tensions with the Ugyhur's also rose and there were allegations of cultural cleansing of the latter.

The PRC also had skirmishes with the Russians who were supporting the East Turkistan Republic movement. However, they have used a heavy hand on the minorities and there are allegations of human right abuses. The latest is the series of re-education camps for Ugyhur's wherein more than a million people are incarcerated.

The story of Xinjiang is thus one of how the Chinese regime in the garb of three dynastic rules of the Han, Tang and Qing has argued that the region is part of China. Culturally the region is very diverse being earlier inhabited by the Mongols in the north and the Turks in the south. It has no cultural affinity with the other provinces of China. Nevertheless, the classic strategy of change in the demographic profile to increase the population of Han Chinese is what has enabled the regime to assimilate this region into China. This is clearly a form of territorial expansion since the Chinese have usurped land and rather than maintain its multicultural identity, changed it completely.

What is also interesting is that they have suppressed the religious freedom of the Ugyhur's through the internment camps set up, in what they term as re-education. No prayers are allowed in the mosques of the region and the even growing of beards is prohibited. It is one of the most policed regions of the world, almost akin to North Korea. This policy has been put in place on account of fear of terrorist activities in the region. The Chinese are aware of the volatile situation in the neighbouring regions like Iran, Afghanistan and Central Asian Republics which could foster unrest in the region too. It is with this threat in view that the Chinese were one of the first countries to establish ties with the Taliban when it came to power in Afghanistan in August 2021. They agreed on providing aid in lieu on no interference in the Xinjiang region.

China's expansionism in Xinjiang is fuelled by the rich mineral resources of the region. The word "Xinjiang" in mandarin means "new territory" and for China this is a new frontier. It also provides access to Central Asia and then to Europe.

CHAPTER SIX

Capture of the Roof of the World

Before we get into the phase of the annexation of Tibet, it is important to dwell on the history of this region. While it has a rich history from the pre-historic period, that era remains largely undocumented. The actual documentation began with the introduction of Buddhism from India in the 6th century.

Subsequently, the Tibetan empire led by the Yarlung dynasty established itself in the 7th century and continued its reign until the middle of the 9th century. The empire started in 618 AD by the 33rd king of the Yarlung dynasty Songsten Gampo expanded and even covered regions beyond the Tibetan plateau. During its peak, it covered the entire provinces of Xingjiang, Sichuan, Gansu, Yunnan, Ladakh, Kashmir, Gilgit as well as the current countries of Tajikistan and Uzbekistan. Moreover, the dynasty also demarcated borders on more than one occasion with the Tang dynasty that was ruling China. It was during the Tibetan empire reign that Buddhism spread in the region with the first emperor having embraced it.

With the assassination of 42nd King Langdarma in 842AD, the empire saw its prominence go. The assassination is attributed to a monk who is said to have avenged the regime of terror perpetuated by the King on the monasteries. Then began a fight for succession with the advent of the era of fragmentation. This period witnessed rebellions and civil war and a period of uncertainty. This led to the rise of regional satraps who ruled over their respective provinces. Broadly there were 10 major provinces stretching from Zanskar, present Kashmir in the west to Amdo, currently Central China in the west.

It was after this fragmentation era that Tibet was conquered by the Mongols in 1240. Subsequently in 1244, the first historical influence of the Yuan dynasty, a province under the Mongol empire, was witnessed as the region was ruled by them for a period of over 100 years. However, the region was administered by the Bureau of Buddhist and Tibetan Affairs which provided autonomy over religious, political and legal affairs. The structural and administrative control however vested with the Mongols through the Yuan rulers. This is also called the Sakya era since Sakya Pandita was the first Viceroy of Central Tibet and the Sakya lamas were appointed subsequently.

However, the country became independent in the 14th century and was ruled for nearly three centuries by some noble houses. It was in the 17th century that a senior lama of the Gelug school, the Dalai Lama became the Head of State. It was through the Tumed Mongols that the Dalai Lamas established their power in Tibet. The 5th Dalai Lama, Lobsang Gyatso who established effective political power over Central Tibet. However, this was possible only after internal strife resulting in suppression of the other schools of Buddhism like Kangyu and Jonang. He also constructed the Potala Palace, the seat of power in Lhasa.

However, in the 18th century, Tibet was once again overrun, this time by the Qing dynasty. It remained under occupation till the beginning of the 20th century after which the dynasty collapsed. They established their power through the local imperial residents known as the ambans. They also used the classic *"divide and rule"* strategy between the two highest Lamas, the Dalai and Panchen Lama to establish their hegemony. The Qings stationed troops in the capital and assimilated some of the eastern Tibetan empire provinces into their own. There were continuous skirmishes and an air of political uncertainty hung over the political future of Tibet.

In 1840, the Dogra Kingdom under General Zorawar Singh attacked Tibet with a view to increasing the empire. However, while they captured Taklakot, near the border with Nepal, they were repulsed by the Tibetan reinforcements in 1841. The Tibetans then sought to capture Ladakh but were in turn defeated leading to the signing of the Treaty of Chushul.

The British influence over Tibet increased from 1900 onwards as they tried to assert themselves over the region. They tested the waters especially in show of strengths with both the Qing dynasty and the Tsarist Russia. Colonel Younghusband led a British expedition to wane the influence of the Russians and he signed some treaties. The Qings noticing this show of power by the British and the Russians tried to integrate Tibet into China.

Subsequently in 1912, after the collapse of the Qing dynasty, Tibet won its independence with all the ambans and external influences deported. There was a Sino-Tibetan war in 1932 wherein the Tibetans, trying to expand to the erstwhile Tibetan empire were defeated by an army comprising both Han and Muslim soldiers. After that, barring the British who stationed their trade emissaries, no other country had any contact with independent Tibet until the Chinese invasion.

The Chinese civil war saw the establishment of Communist Rule in the country in 1949 under Chairman Mao Zedong. The new rulers lost no time in trying to integrating Tibet into China. They attacked the Chomdo region in October, 1950 and forced some Tibetan representatives in Beijing to sign a 17 point agreement that established their suzerainty over Tibet. Moreover, they also captured the Amdo and Kham region integrating them into their provinces and stationed a large number of troops in central Tibet.

The US entered the fray in 1956-57 through the CIA which was supporting the rebels trying to dislodge Chinese rule but it did not succeed since most the air dropped Tibetan resistance leaders were captured and never seen again. The Chinese on the other hand were supported by the Russian in their military hardware as they bombed Lhasa and other towns of Tibet. In 1959, the Chinese were on the verge of capture of the Dalai Lama when a group of Tibetans surrounded the palace and facilitated his escape to India. The Chinese after occupying Tibet destroyed most the monasteries in the region and vandalized its cultural sites.

The Chinese have subsequently ruled Tibet with an iron hand including changing its demographic profile by settling largely the Han Chinese. This has been a classic ploy even in the Xinjiang province wherein the original denizens are then outnumbered thereby facilitating any crackdowns. There were riots in Tibet during 2008 against the Chinese rule but it was dealt with a heavy hand. However, with little information disseminated out of Tibet, the autocratic rule has been enforced strongly by the Chinese.

What does all this narrative tell about the Chinese occupation of Tibet? The Communist regime has been peddling the story that since the Yuan under the Mongols and the Qing dynasty ruled over Tibet, the province is part of China. Moreover, they also point to the tacit understanding of the British, the 17 point agreement that was signed by some Tibetan representatives in Beijing and the general acceptance of other western powers that Tibet is part of China.

The core reasons why Tibet cannot be considered as part of China is the cultural, social, religious and linguistic identity of the people who inhabited the region at the time of independence. While they were ruled over twice by Chinese dynasties, they were never integrated as a province despite the efforts of the Qing rulers towards the end and maintained their identity. This disparity only increased after the Chinese revolution that installed an atheist Communist regime, distinct from the largely Buddhist Tibet.

The strategy to change the demographic profile of the region by rendering the Tibetans to a minority is a ploy used by China even in Xinjiang. It is thus a territorial expansion akin to the German strategy in WWII to annex territories to settle their population.

CHAPTER SEVEN

Two pronged war with India

Ladakh and the annexation of Aksai Chin

Ladakh has a strategic location as it is bordered by Tibet in the east, Xinjiang in the north, Gilgit Baltistan in the west, Kashmir in south west and Himachal in the south. It was the hub of the trade routes between these regions. Geographically, it is ensconced between the Siachen glacier and the Himalayas and is an extension of the Tibetan plateau.

Ancient history saw the region, which was sandwiched between Kashmir and Tibet and ruled by the Zhangzhung kingdom being overrun by powers from both sides. In middle history, the Maryul dynasty established itself for nearly five centuries but the region then came under the control of both Mongols and the Mughals. Islam spread to this region at this point of time. Towards the end of the 17th century, the region sided with Bhutan in a dispute with Tibet and this resulted in an invasion by the latter. The Mughals came to the rescue but had to be paid off. The region then signed a treaty with the Tibetans for peace but this severely restricted their sovereignty. In 1834, General Zorawar Singh annexed Ladakh into the Sikh empire but the latter lost a battle to the British who then got the region under its suzerainty as a princely state. However, until independence of India, some Tibetan leaders still harboured ambitions to take over this region.

Coming to Aksai Chin, the region which lies between Tibet and the Tarim Basin in Xinjiang while being inhospitable, had its strategic importance. It was open throughout the year for transiting trading caravans or military forces to cross between the two regions. Even the name has its controversies with the pro Chinese historians translating Chin to mean "*Chinese*" while others attributing it to mean "*a pass*", which is not difficult to fathom from the use of the region. Even after the British capture of the Ladakh from the Sikhs, this region was never demarcated and the formers contact with the Qing dynasty to settle borders was not reciprocated.

It was then that the British cartographers jumped into the fray and the entire controversy is stated to have stemmed from that. William Johnson and subsequently John Ardagh, first drew lines which showed Aksai Chin as part of British India. However, based on some discussions with Chinese officials, a British counsel in Kashgar, Macartney and Claude Mc Donald, proposed another line known as the Macartney-Macdonald line which showed the region as part of China. This was premised on the Karakoram being a natural border. However, when these maps were sent to the Qing dynasty, they never acknowledged it and there was no agreement. Moreover, with the collapse of the Qing, the Britishers themselves started recognizing the Johnson-Ardagh line which had Aksai Chin as part of British India.

After independence, India stuck to the British position of the Johnson line being the boundary. However, strangely all this was done only on maps and there was little military establishment at the ground level for safeguarding this border. Using this lacunae, the Chinese built a road in 1950 running through Aksai Chin since their access was less of a constraint than the Indian side which had to traverse the higher Karakoram ranges to reach it. The lack of presence at the ground level was exposed when India came to know of this road only after seven years in 1957. India nevertheless, still sought some diplomatic solution to this and restated its claim on Aksai Chin to which the Chinese did not respond. It was a situation in which neither wanted to give up on their territorial claims nor antagonize the other. It was the beginning of a cold war within overtly warm relations.

The Ladakh theatre saw a jump in the skirmishes between both countries. However, the turning point was when Dalai Lama was granted asylum by India in 1959 after he escaped the crackdown in Lhasa. After this the posturing shifted to one of antagonism and it was clear that things would give way. On October, 1959, a clash took place at Kongka pass when nine Indian frontier guards died. The situation went downhill with the dispute stretching to the Mcmahon line on the eastern front. Chinese premier Chou En Lai in 1960 did informally suggest a swap deal wherein India gave up its claim on Aksai Chin in return for China recognizing NEFA as part of India. However, India was adamant that both the regions were hers since they were part of the British territory at the time of independence. However, the Chinese claim over Aksai Chin in 1960 went even beyond the Macartney-MacDonald line and it had occupied most of this region.

This tense situation along the border led to what India adopted was its Forward Policy at the end of `1961. The strategy was to have posts which defended India's claims on the territory and not allowing the Chinese to advance and forcing them to vacate the posts they had occupied. While there was limited success in this strategy, it provoked the Chinese who then began war mongering by sending signals of India's expansionist plans including on Tibet and the need to assert their control over Aksai Chin. The Chinese leadership timed its intervention to perfection since the Cuban missile crisis loomed in the background and this ensured the Soviets were willing to be a neutral party to this dispute. Moreover, the relations between India and the US had plummeted after the incorporation of the State of Goa into the Indian Union. The Chinese were thus left with an open invite to annex Aksai Chin and NEFA.

The build up to the actual war was in the form of skirmishes, the first of which one in June, 1962 when a dozen Chinese troops lost their lives. Then in July 1962, they surrounded an Indian post but backed off. In the interim period until the actual war in October, 1962, there were hardly any diplomatic efforts worth the name to talk bilaterally and resolve the issue. Both sides cringed in taking the first step and in such a situation, no third country interlocutors were also approached. It was a strange situation with China playing up the ante about India preparing for a full-fledged war while Indian policy makers and defence officials still did not believe that China would go to war. To sum up, it was a diplomatic fiasco coupled with the Cuban Missile crisis that led to the actual war.

The actual Chinese attack came on 19 October, 1962 when they attacked through the Chip Chap valley in Aksai Chin. They were soon in control of most of Aksai Chin including the Galwan valley and Pang Tso lake. A fierce battle occurred along the Rezang La ridge. The Indian forces hit by the magnitude of the aggression lost many men and had to withdraw. The Chinese who were already in control of much of Aksai Chin had gone much further below the Macartney Macdonald line. With a lull in the war, Premier Zhou En Lai sent two messages to the Indian PM for mutual withdrawal of forces and settlement of the boundary but the first proposal was rejected by India since this was a military aggression. Due to this stalemate, the war resumed on 18 November and the Chinese attacked Chushul and Rezang la inflicting heavy casualties on the Indian side, who were forced to retreat further. A unilateral ceasefire was declared by China on 19 November. While the west including

Americans made some statements on the Chinese aggression, more worried on the expansion of communism, they did little on the ground to help Indian forces in combat. Even the non-aligned Members apart from Egypt to some extent, kept quiet and did not condemn the Chinese aggression. It was a colossal diplomatic failure and India had paid a heavy price. Pakistan had made some overtures to India for having a joint stand on the demarcation of the Northern frontiers with China. India, however, did not reciprocate and the Pakistanis then had no option but to formalize a treaty with China in December, 1962 ceding some territory north of the Karakoram's to the Chinese to buy peace. It was from this point onwards that they became diplomatically closer to China. The Russians did sign an agreement for supply of aircraft but no air power was used in the war. This could have been another tactical mistake by India since in these high altitude terrains the equipment for ground forces was inadequate.

There were subsequent clashes when Chinese troops patrolled and occupied parts of Pangong Tso. A bloody hand to hand combat ensured in the Galwan valley in 2020 where both sides lost a number of their men. The standoffs continued even into 2021 with a tense border situation and the Chinese building some strong structures with a view to permanent occupation of the region. The Galwan incident was also interesting since it came after India withdrew from an important economic and trade engagement known as the Regional Comprehensive Economic Partnership (RCEP) in which both were participants.

CHAPTER EIGHT

North East Frontier Agency (NEFA) or Arunachal Pradesh

Arunachal Pradesh was in ancient history ruled by the Monpa kingdom in the Northwest and the Sutia kings of Assam in the south. The influence of Hinduism and Buddhism is evident during these reigns. The British established agreements with the natives during 1912-13 to form the North Eastern Frontier Tracts which was later renamed as the North East Frontier Agency (NEFA).

Major Jenkins, an agent posted in the region said that the Tawang region was part of Tibet. Moreover, British records of the 19th century show Tawang as part of Tibet given the importance of its monastery. However, in 1913, a tripartite agreement was signed between the Britain, China and Tibet on demarcating the territory. What is crucial in this agreement is that the Qing dynasty had collapsed and China did not have effective control over Tibet which became independent. China later did not agree to the demarcation in this agreement but the question is on the locus standi of China given that Tibet was independent at that point of time. Foreign Secretary Macmohan then settled the boundary with Tibet and the line was south of the Himalayas which was taken as a natural boundary. Tawang town was placed in British India but this continued to be administered by Tibetan officials until World War II after which the British took over control of this town too.

After independence, India during patrolling found some of the natural boundaries such as ridges north of the Macmahon line and claimed it as its territory. This further complicated the boundary dispute and provide the Chinese with a lever to aggravate it.

The 1959 Tibetan uprising and India granting asylum to the Dalai Lama was the last straw for the Chinese. They went on an overdrive to project India's strategy for reclaiming Tibet. The first of the skirmishes was in August 1959 when an Indian prisoner was taken in Longju. In 1960, China was willing to drop its demand for NEFA in lieu of Aksai Chin but India stuck to its position of both territories being part of

India. This further angered the Chinese who believed that India had ambitions on Tibet.

As in the case of Aksai Chin, the Forward Policy of India to safeguard its territories precipitated the situation. In June 1962, India established the Dhola post in the Namka Chu valley which was south of the Thaga La ridge. However, in September, Chinese forces descended down the ridge and occupied the Indian post. Their access was easier than that of the Indians and the skirmishes went throughout the month. India then tried to secure another strategic point known as the Yamsto La but failed to do so due to the strength in numbers of the Chinese. However, China was reinforcing its end and it was clear that they were building for an all- out war premised on their two fold thinking that India had ambitions on Tibet and its forward policy meant to push back the Chinese on both the Aksai Chin and NEFA fronts.

The war began on 20 October with the Chinese attacking the Namka Chu Valley and flanking the Indian forces who were forced to retreat into Bhutan. Another attack took place at Walong on 22 October wherein despite fierce resistance, the Indians were forced to retreat. Tawang also came under attack and was evacuated. This was the first phase of the war after which there was a pause when premier Zhou En Lai tried to get India to the negotiating table. However, when that failed, the second phase of the conflict began in November.

During this second phase, the Chinese started their attacks on 17 November, 1962 to capture Se La and Bomdi La. They did not make a frontal attack but a flanking one by occupying some the supply routes to Se La such as Thembang. With the fall of Se La, the defences in Bomdi La were also overrun with relative ease and the Chinese pushed southwards. The entire military success was hinged on the strategy of multi-pronged attacks, flanking maneuvers, encirclement, cutting off supply lines, number advantage and better ammunition and artillery.

This multiple front attack is compared in Chinese military journals to the 1950 attack on the US Marine Division in the Chosin Reservoir battle of the Korean war. Moving southwards, the Chinese came to the outskirts of Tezpur in Assam. The evacuation of civilians from Tezpur was also carried out as they were shifted to south of the Brahmaputra. The unilateral ceasefire then came about on 19 November, 1962.

However, the Chinese retreated from NEFA to the area north of the McMahon line. There is a lot of speculation as to why the Chinese went back after capturing the territory on the eastern sector. These range from theories such as China wanting to teach India a lesson to the fact that diplomatic pressure was mounting on them from the west who were scared of communist expansion. Some also say that the retreat may have been precipitated by the situation back home with the great famine while others also mention possibility of a large scale war with India if they had hung onto this territory.

It is important to look at the key outcomes from these two conflicts with India. China's strategy is to link the entire dispute by claiming what it believes is Tibet's territory as part of its own. It has used the history of the Tibetan empire to showcase that the regions on the western and eastern front with India were disputed. More, importantly it took advantage of India's ground level absence to occupy territory such as Aksai Chin and then claim it as its own. Of course Aksai Chin was strategically important for it to construct a road from Tibet to Xinjiang. In the NEFA region, it disputed all the agreements made by the Britishers with Tibet claiming that any agreement must have the backing of China. This is the classic nibbling strategy based on interpretations wherein it can claim larger tracts of lands and thereby fructify its Lebensraum. On the NEFA front, its withdrawal still remains a mystery but as discussed earlier, it could be a mix of many factors including international condemnation.

CHAPTER NINE

South China Sea on fire

The South China Sea dispute is a classic example wherein the dragon has taken on many nations in a multi-pronged dispute. These include Brunei, Indonesia, Malaysia, Taiwan and Vietnam. Some third parties such as South Korea and India have also faced the brunt of the Chinese.

The entire dispute which is territorial has assumed larger proportions primarily on account of the both the sea being a crucial navigation route and its potential oil reserves. These waters are rich in marine fauna and some of the disputes also pertain to the fishing rights. Strategic considerations played a crucial part in terms of maritime security for shipping lines. More than half of fuel related imports and nearly half of China's overall trade pas through the South China Sea.

The key territories that are at the centre of this dispute are the Natuna Islands, Paracel Islands, Scarborough Shoal and Spratly Islands. While some of the disputes predate even the Communist regime of China, things began to get heated in 2013 when China started its massive exercise of island building. During the period 2014-2016, China managed to station military equipment on the disputed islands. While purists may argue that both Philippines and Vietnam were also engaged in reclaiming land, their exercise was not of the gargantuan scale of the Chinese and it was more on a defensive scale.

The dispute over Paracel and Spratly began in 1939 when Imperial Japan occupied it. The islands were used for military purposes and no one laid claim over it at that point of time.

However, it is believed that the French colonialists had gone to these islands. With the defeat of the Japanese and the 1951 Treaty of San Francisco, they had to surrender these islands.

The Paracel and Spratly islands were considered part of Vietnam under the Geneva Accords of 1954. However, with the Vietnam war in 1974 and an imminent victory of the North Vietnamese, China moved in shrewdly to take advantage of the situation in the Paracel islands. With the US showing disinterest in intervening, after having literally bitten the dust in the war, the timing of China could not have been more opportune. The Chinese navy showed its prowess and defeated the Vietnamese and occupied the Paracels. There were some ugly confrontations over these islands. A South Korean navy destroyer strayed into the 12 nautical mile territorial waters. However, the reasoning given was that it was avoiding a typhoon in the region.

As far as the Spratly islands were concerned, Philippines laid claim to it in 1978. Malaysia too joined the fray and this became a three way contest. China used a smart tactic taking a mandate from the Intergovernmental Oceanographic Commission to establish observation posts in one of the reefs.

Piggybacking on this, they engaged in battle with Vietnam in 1988 and won over the Johnson reef. The Chinese also confronted the Philippines over the Mischief reef of the Spratly. In December, 2020, the US destroyer John McCain is said to have been confronted by China near the islands but the US navy refuted any such incident. Later in March, 2021; Chinese fishing boats had gone to the Whitsun reef, an area claimed by Philippines which lodged a protest.

With Paracel virtually in control of China, they set their ambitions on Spratly which was still being occupied by other powers. In 2013, they began island building to garner greater control and shift the balance of power.

Another area of contention was the Scarborough shoal which was being used by Chinese fishing boats. In 2012, when Philippines challenged it, the Chinese took over these waters

A nine dash line which was recognized by the Communist regime lies at the centre of this dispute. The Republic of China prior to the current government had a eleven dash line. These were basically lines and dots establishing Chinese sovereignty over the waters of the

South China Sea. It overlaps with the Exclusive Economic Zone (EEZ) of a number of countries like Brunei, Indonesia, Malaysia, Philippines, Taiwan and Vietnam. In July, 2020, even Australia challenged China's right over the South China Sea questioning the validity of the nine dash. The relationship between Australia and China plummeted after that. The only countries who are actually supporting China are Cambodia and Laos but in case of the former, it is largely a result of the anti-Vietnamese sentiment.

The Chinese strategy has been denoted as *"salami slicing"*. It has forced the western powers, chiefly the United States to conduct freedom of navigation exercises which has further upset the frayed nerves of the Chinese. Despite an arbitration tribunal decision against China's maritime claims with Philippines, they have not honoured the decision. `The salami slicing is the nibbling strategy wherein China tests its adversary by a provocative action and then backs off if the response is tough. It is almost like a game of attrition which tries to unsettle the other side. Some analysts have pointed to the tactic being a series of small slicing moves which take the opponent by surprise leaving them with a choice of either ignoring or risking full-fledged confrontation.

Whatever be the judgement, the Chinese tactic has been successful in expanding its territorial claims. Unlike the World Wars, the Chinese have used the concept of Lebensraum quite smartly in the South China Sea. They have asserted their power only for the final kill, after the salami tactics have had the effect of unnerving the other protagonists. It has also given them an opportunity to beef up their naval prowess, an important ingredient of their overall global hegemony.

Another strategy attributed to China in this region is the cabbage tactic. This is akin to surrounding an island with an arsenal consisting of fishing boats, patrol vessels, coast guard and naval battleships thus keeping out any contenders. The name comes from the peels of security just like the cabbage leaves. It has worked well for China which has complete control of Paracel and has been successfully isolating potential claimants by a multi-pronged show of force.

CHAPTER TEN

Sikkim

Sikkim had historical ties with Tibet, Nepal and Bhutan both on account of the many wars fought as well as trade. Buddhism is said to have be introduced by Rinpoche in the 9th century. The Lepchas, Limbus and the Magars were the predominant tribes of the region at the advent of the Chogyal kingdom in the 17th century. This was when Sikkim became monarchy. The Bhutia's came from Tibet to settle in the region. The Chogyal's were consecrated by the three Great Lamas and had to rely on Tibetan soldiers to subdue dissension from the Limbus and Magars. The Bhutanese invaded the region but with the help of the Tibetans, the monarchy was restores. However, during the subsequent rule, they were overrun by the Gurkhas from Nepal. However, they were repulsed again with the help of the Tibetans with the Qing dynasty establishing their control over the region for the first time. However, the Chinese did not control the region for long.

With the advent of the British rule, Sikkim was forced to ally themselves with the former in order to defend itself against the Gurkha kingdom. The British managed to defeat the Gurkhas but their relationship with the monarchy soured on account of their taxation of the Morang region. Based on an agreement with the Qing dynasty, the British took over Sikkim as a protectorate and was even granted the status of a princely state. At the time of independence of India, the newly formed government did not try to integrate the state into its territory. However, there was an intervention on the request of the monarchy to quell a rebellion that sought among things the accession to India. Sikkim became a protectorate of the Indian government.

The Chinese had always being eyeing Sikkim since the Qing dynasty had control over it for a brief period of time. On a high after defeating India in the 1962 battle and seizing an opportunity to expand their territory, they tried to intrude into Sikkim through Nathu La and Cho La in 1967. These battles which were fought in September and October of that year saw the Indian forces repulse the Chinese attack and destroy many of their bunkers. These setbacks put the Chinese ambition of usurping Sikkim on hold as they analysed how the internal situation in the region panned out.

On the internal front, there were subsequent rebellions against the Chogyals, and on the request of the Sikkimese Prime Minister to integrate Sikkim into India, the latter intervened and took over the territory. A referendum was held which voted to remove the monarchy paving way for Sikkim to be part of India. Based on the constitutional amendment, Sikkim became a State of India in 1975.

The Chinese efforts in Sikkim did not fructify but given their thought process, they would continue to look for opportunities. However, with Sikkim becoming part of India, it would not be an easy task.

CHAPTER ELEVEN

Bhutan

While the early history of Bhutan is not well documented and is mired in speculation, the introduction of Tibetan Buddhism in the 9th century with the fleeing of many lamas from Tibet is the first vindicated evidence. Buddhism flourished in the region with influences of various teachers who came from both India and Tibet. By the 14th century a powerful Gelugpa school of Buddhism that flourished in Tibet forced many to flee to Bhutan thus establishing the Lhapa and the Drukpa sub sects of the Kargyupa school took roots in the regions until the 17th century.

The Drukpa monk Ngawang Namgyal, known as the 1st Zhabdrung, became the spiritual leader in Bhutan as he managed to stave off the invasions from Tibet in the 17th century. He held firm and even had good relations with the rulers of Cooch Behar, Nepal and Ladakh. He had established a well oiled administrative structure dividing the kingdoms into Dzongs along with a legal code known as the Tsa Yig. After his death, his successors managed to hold into the kingdom even having conflict with both Sikkim and Tibet in the 18th century.

Bhutan had a close relationship with Ladakh and even supported them in their war with Tibet. They were granted some enclaves near Mount Kailash for setting up of monasteries. This remained under their control until 1959 when communist China annexed Tibet. Bhutan had also managed to exercise control over Cooch Behar in the latter's conflict with the Mughals.

However, with the coming over of the British in 1772, things changed and Bhutan lost control over Cooch Behar. A peace treaty was signed with the East India company in 1774 but a lot of territories had to be ceded including that of Bengal Duars. With boundary disputes galore, the Britishers also tried to take over Assam Duars in 1841. The territories were lost during the Duar wars of 1864-65.

There were a lot of internal rivalries in the region before the collapse of the Zhabdrung system and the ascendancy of a monarchy under Ugyen Wangchuck in 1907. This was supported by the Britishers who wanted peace in the region for exercising influence over Tibet. It was during this time that China had nursed some ambitions over Tibet. However, the Treaty of Punakha which was signed with the British put paid to their hopes as they did not want to take on the colonial empire.

The monarchy continued with the Wangchuk family and there was another Friendship Treaty signed in August 1949 with India which ensured that the latter would not interfere in internal affairs of the country.

With the communist takeover in China and the latter's annexation of Tibet, Bhutan was forced to come close to India. They undertook land reforms and modernization, much with Indian aid including building up of roads. Despite the internal strife, the country has remained on the growth trajectory. In the 1962 Sino-India war, they provided territory for the Indian troops to escape the Chinese onslaught. However, with India's defeat in the war, Bhutan has been trying to adopt a neutral policy. They also took membership of the UN. While maintaining a close diplomatic relationship with India, they continue to walk a tightrope ensuring that they remain a buffer state between China and India.

With the Bhutan-Tibet border not having been clearly demarcated, China post annexation of Tibet has been using the border dispute as a lever to nibble away territory. The influx of Tibetan refugees into Bhutan post the downfall of Lhasa has seen relationship with China plummet. China has laid claim to significant parts of Bhutan under the pretext that it was part of Tibet.

The dispute began with 2017 in Doklam where China was building a road into what Bhutan claims as its territory. India entered the fray and blocked the building of this road. There was a tense standoff between troops from both sides. The Chinese are believed to have continued the construction of the road. In June, 2020, they also claimed that the Sakteng wildlife sanctuary was disputed and no grant could be given to Bhutan for its preservation. China has thus being using its conventional strategy of raking up issues with a view to nibbling territory and staking their claim to a larger empire.

CHAPTER TWELVE

Central Asian Borders

The border dispute between China and some of the Central Asian countries traces back to the times of the Russian empires expansion into Central Asia including the Lake Zysan region. The boundaries between the Russian Empire and the Qing dynasty were demarcated vide the 1860 Convention of Peking, 1864 Treaty of Tarbagatai and the 1870 Treaty of Uliassuhai.

Moreover, the struggle between Britain and Russia in this region added to the complexity and the borders were re-demarcated. With China not being a party to these agreements, the Sino-Soviet borders were undefined.

With the disintegration of the Soviet Union in 1991, Tajikistan inherited this disputed border. It was only after agreements with China in 1999 and 2002 which were ratified in 2011 that some territories were ceded to China to establish peace in the region. However, the situation is still not completely defused since China still made a claim in June 2020 which was rejected by both Russia and Tajikistan.

Kazakhstan inherited the same legacy from the undemarcated borders as a result of the British-Russian rivalry as well as the erstwhile Russian empire treaties with the Qing dynasty. The Kazakhs after independence signed a treaty with China in 1994 by ceding some territory. Additional agreements were signed in 1997 and 1998 which was followed by setting up of joint commissions to demarcate the borders. The process was hence relatively more peaceful than that of Tajikistan.

In the case of Kyrgystan, the situation was the same with the undemarcated borders at the time of independence. However, the natural boundary of the Tien Shan mountains presented a lesser challenge when the demarcation was carried out in 1996. However, the internal Tulip Revolution prevented a formal agreement since there was opposition to these demarcations. An agreement was signed in 2009 wherein some territories were swapped.

While the situation in Central Asian has not been as daunting as other regions, China still continues to harbor ambitions with smaller countries like Tajikistan. They have been looking for loopholes in the political governance and could very well raise the issue later seeking more territory. However, the interference of Russia would always be a stumbling block in any heightened territorial ambition.

While the Central Asian Republics have not had the type of border disputes as seen with other countries, the presence of Russia has been a big factor in checking their Lebensraum. The erstwhile Soviet Union has close ties with all these three Central Asian Republics which has borders with Xinjiang. More than a quarter of the population in all these three countries also speak Russian which is one of the official languages too.

It is only in the case of Tajikistan that the situation is still not completely defused and China has been flexing its muscles at the border. There have been standoffs too and China has been smart trying to probe any weaknesses that it could exploit. This is very similar to the South China sea tactics of salami slicing. However, the presence of Russia does act as some deterrent.

CHAPTER THIRTEEN

Taiwan

Taiwan was under Dutch colonial rule in the 17th century. However, a loyalist of the erstwhile Ming dynasty, Konxinga invaded the island and defeated the Dutch in the decisive battle of the Fort of Zeelandia. He then established the Kingdom of Tungning in 1662.

They then resorted to the classic strategy of settlement of the Han Chinese thereby changing the demographic profile and marginalizing the original denizens of the island. Confucian temples were established and Chinese language schools were opened.

In the ensuring battle, the Qing dynasty attacked Tungning and defeated the Ming loyalists in the battle of Penghu. This was the beginning of the Qing rule though they did not initially show any great intent to make it part of their empire. Subsequently, the Qing's understood the strategic importance of the island when the Japanese and the French staked their claims. The island was rich in natural resources and a gateway to the mainland. It was then that the Qing's made Taiwan a part of the Fujian province.

The Japanese entered the fray and after winning the Sino-Japanese war in 1895 annexed the island along with Penghu. They used the island for supply of rice and sugar as well as a military base to attack South East Asia. Taiwan became a manufacturing hub for war time material and it is said that this exceeded the agricultural production of the island. They even implemented their education policy in the island with Japanese language and worship being made mandatory.

With the defeat of the Japanese in World War II, Republic of China took over the island. They established the Taiwan Provincial Government with the pro Chinese challenging this proclamation. The Republic forces were however defeated in the mainland in 1949 by the Communists and had to retreat to Taiwan including the islands of Kinmen, Matsu and

Wuqui. Around 2 million refugees came to the island from the Nationalist Party. Many of the Japanese settlers were also deported from the island. Taiwan also lost its United Nations seat and was expelled in 1971 as it refused to accept a joint seat with Communist China. In 1979, the US also recognized China over Taiwan.

The Kuomintang ruled the island until 1980 after which democratic reforms were ushered in. Taiwan's economy subsequently grew. The impressive growth which made it one of the four Asian tigers was riding on the back of the boom in the electronic hardware and semi-conductor industry.

However, the Communist regime never recognized Taiwan as an independent country and had been eyeing to make it part of China. The first Taiwan crisis happened in August, 1954 when China attacked the islands of Kinmen and Matsu with an eventual aim of capturing Taiwan. The United States after having borne the brunt of communist China in the Korean war, sent its seventh fleet to defend Taiwan. Communist China managed to capture Yijiangshan islands but the US upped its tempo stating that it would not hesitate to use nuclear weapons. This nuclear brinkmanship is what brought the crisis to an end. However, it provided the communists a rationale for development of their own nuclear weapons.

The second Taiwan crisis began in August, 1958 when the Chinese attacked Dongding Islands which were under the control of the Nationalist Taiwan government. The attack was through an attempt at landing. However, they suffered casualties as many vessels were sunk. While the US 7th fleet again provided support to defend the passage through the Taiwan straits which was being bombarded through Chinese artillery including on the island of Kinmen. This was also the crisis which saw a lot of aerial battles. The US provided its lethal air to air sidewinder missiles to Taiwan which tilted the aerial combat in favour of the Nationalists. They shot down a number of Mig fighters which the Russians had supplied to the Chinese. While the crisis was over by December, 1958, there was a strange arrangement of firing on alternate days. This went on until 1979 when the crisis eventually ended. The Americans once again used the bogey of a nuclear weapon use in this standoff.

The third crisis in 1995 was due to the testing carried out by China in the waters around Taiwan. It was also a pressure tactic to prevent a China hawk President Lee Teng-hui from winning the Taiwanese elections in 1996. However, the US which was first antagonistic to President Lee reversed its stance due to domestic pressure. The US sent its largest fleet to the region with a view to defend Taiwan. While the situation was tense, the US presence was the deterrence for China which had earlier signaled its ambition to take over Taiwan. President Lee won the elections primarily due to the Chinese faux paux in raking up the issue. The current incumbent Tsai Ing-Wen faced a similar situation. She was the first elected female Head of State of Taiwan in 2016. In the run up to the 2020 elections, China started its sabre rattling given her stance of being a firm opponent of any unification with the mainland. She opposed the call of Chinese premier Xi Jinping of *"One country, two systems"* policy stating that Taiwan would not support it. Her proximity to the US administration has really irked the mainland who did not want a 3rd country to be involved in this dispute. Moreover, in all the crisis involving the two countries, it is the intervention of US that upset the applecart of China in annexing Taiwan.

Another school of thought on China's ambition to annex Taiwan is largely economic. It stems from the manufacturing powerhouse that Taiwan has become as a result of its economic policies. When one looks at the electronic hardware sector, the Taiwan Semiconductor Manufacturing Company (TSMC), established in 1987 is the leading global player in semi-conductor manufacturing. The semi-conductor is the heart of all electronic devices such as mobile phones. Many of the Chinese manufacturers of mobile phones are dependent on TSMC for their products as also from the designs where US apart from Japan and South Korea have prowess. Therefore, China despite being the largest producer of electronic goods, has had limited success in backward integration despite investing heavily in chip manufacturing. Annexation of Taiwan would provide it the necessary missing link in the value chain. However, on the design side, the US sanctions would also affect them but there are alternate suppliers and the Chinese are masters of copying with non-existent patent enforcement laws. It is interesting to note that with the start of the Taiwan crisis, even TSMC has been actively shifting its facilities of manufacturing critical parts to Japan.

China has repeatedly signaled its intent to capture Taiwan and integrate it under the one China policy. There was a 1992 meeting of officials from both countries on the issue of enhancing relationship. Both sides however have different interpretations of this meeting which is known as the *"1992 Consensus"*. China believes that the consensus was on unification while Taiwan has a contrary opinion. Even Xi Jinping made a proposition for a *"One Country Two Systems"* for eventual unification under the

One China Policy. This was rejected by Taiwan which has also been supporting the protestor's right to freedom in Hong Kong. All this has raised the animosity levels between the two nations.

China has repeatedly raised the ante, expressing its frustration in trying to cow down the current regime in Taiwan by diplomatic pressure. The ploy has been the traditional tactics of creating tension and putting pressure on the Taiwanese armed forces by sending in naval ships and air planes. The latter has been forced to scramble its jets and ships to respond to the threat. However, with the enhanced military build-up by China, there is a real threat of the situation escalating out of hand. With China slowly matching upto the military prowess of the US, things could really get ugly if sanity does not prevail. Moreover, with the slew of measures such as suppression of the pro-democracy movement in Hong Kong, curbing of dissent in Tibet and the temporary disappearance of many mainland celebrities after they made some statements not palatable to the Communist Party; the level of mutual confidence between the two countries is fairly low.

The Ukraine crisis of 2022 wherein Russia made its intentions clear to and invaded the former could just be the opportunity the communist regime may be waiting for. With the US and NATO having made bold moves to support Ukraine in the crisis, China played its card smartly by putting forth its support to the Russians with a view to forge an alliance against the west. More importantly, it is almost déjà vu like the Cuban missile crisis during the two front attack on India wherein while the world is focused on the Ukrainian crisis, they could well sneak an attack on its island neighbor. However, with the show of strength by the US destroyers in the Taiwan straits and the possible mining of the straits, it could still be a different story. However, as the Ukraine crisis unfolds, we need to wait and watch.

CHAPTER FOURTEEN

Belt and Road Initiative (BRI)

The Belt and Road Initiative (BRI) has been one of the marquee initiatives of the current Chinese regime and was started in 2013. It seeks to improve connectivity among the countries bordering it. This would improve regional trade, rectify the infrastructural bottlenecks and modernize transport networks in the region.

However, it is also a politically and diplomatically strategic tool that enhances China's clout not only in the region but isolates some of the other powers that influence these regions such as Japan, Russia and the United States. It also seeks to shape the legal, institutional and governance landscape of the region.

There has however, been the hue and cry over the large debts run by the beneficiary governments thereby losing their economic sovereignty. The projects have also stoked sentiments in provinces which are economically poor or where the denizens have been marginalized.

While there is no doubt that the Chinese are known to deliver projects well in time, the consequences of all these big ticket initiatives are not clear. Would it place all these countries at the mercy of the superpower which has all the moolah to give? Can they exercise independent control over these projects and would the local populace actually benefit from these. What is also worrying is that the Chinese in the garb of providing security to their white and blue collar workers have set up their own security apparatus in these projects. They would surely be involved in the maintenance of these projects too and hence could exercise influence over the legal provisions that govern them. Many countries would also be tempted, probably due to some coaxing, to adopt cyber policies, digital regulations and technologies that are similar to that of China. Legislative freedom is something that may be brought into question in such circumstances.

The Chinese have however been engaging bilaterally with the BRI partners to put into effect legislative frameworks. These are focused on investor protection, judicial cooperation and dispute resolution mechanisms. All of these are vital for preserving their interests in the BRI projects for which large investments have been committed.

On the political arena, many of these beneficiary countries, specifically in Central Asia have similar dictatorial regimes as that of China. They are ruled with an iron hand with a weak civil society and no freedom of speech. The human and civil right records are also abysmal. Therefore, it has been to China's advantage that they have not interfered politically too in these regimes preferring the status quo. It is much easier for them to influence and arm twist a central source of power rather than dealing with an array of different voices, a culture alien to the communist regime.

BRI has been an effective tool for China to advance its interest and assert its hegemony not only in the region but globally. It is also a de-facto Sinosraum as it expands its clout, economic, social and security power to these regions. While there are no de-jure territorial claims, the effect could be similar as these frontiers could become economically subservient to them. The classic strategy of some of the dynasties to nibble and chip away at the frontiers is well ensconced in this mammoth initiative.

Many argue that these tactics known as the debt trap diplomacy has forced many countries like Djibouti, Egypt, Ethiopia, Kenya, Papua New Guinea and Sri Lanka to handover their physical assets of the BRI to the Chinese. This gives the latter the screw to virtually put them at their mercy and act as tools to serve China's geopolitical and economic interests.

In the case of Sri Lanka, the Chinese aid provided to develop the Hambantota port ran into some rough weather as Sri Lanka defaulted. This was on account of insufficient revenues generated through traffic at the port despite it being on the main shipping route from the Mallaca straits to the Suez Canal. However, some argue that it was not a debt-trap diplomacy since the Lankans badly needed funds at that point of time and were eyeing to develop the port anyway. The Chinese then took over the port land after the default and hence has an area close from where they can exercise control over the shipping routes from Asia to Africa to Europe.

When one looks at Djibouti, the country is strategically located at the start of the Suez canal. The Chinese have an overseas military base there and could provide them with an effective control over this important waterway.

India did not join the BRI since one of its segments, the China Pakistan Economic Corridor (CPEC) passes through the disputed territory of Gilgit-Baltistan and Pakistan Occupied Kashmir (POK). The CPEC would provide complete road connectivity from the western regions of China and the Central Asian Republics to the Arabian sea at the port of Gwadar. The CPEC ran into rough weather both on account of default on loans by Pakistani agencies as well as opposition by sections in Balochistan who considered it as being exploitative.

The experience of African nations with Chinese investments has also been mixed. While infrastructure has been created, the servicing of loans has been at the heart of the dispute. Since any projects did not the inflexion points of financial viability, it has given rise to a lot of resentment. Chinese control over the natural resources is also a matter of concern for these nations. A déjà vu retreat to the colonial era of exploitation or should be way neo-colonialism.

CHAPTER FIFTEEN

Red bully

China has used its increasing economic and financial muscle to generate clout globally. Understanding the power of the moolah, it has increased funding to international organisations for ensuring that it has control over what they say. As indicated earlier, they have influenced the World Health Organisation (WHO) on not pressurizing them to conduct an internal enquiry on the spread of the COVID virus. This clearly provides fodder to the skeptics who nurse the thought that they might have started this biological warfare. China has curbed a lot of internal dissent and recent turn of events point to the fact that it might be going the way of North Korea in terms of freedom of speech.

We first come to the sporting front. The major organisations and the leagues such as International Olympic Committee (IOC), Association of Tennis Professionals (ATP),

National Basketball Association (NBA) has all literally looked the other way in case of any transgressions. The case of Peng Shuai, the doubles tennis player is a case in point. One of the sporting icons in China, she made some allegations of sexual assault by a high ranking Politburo Member Zhang Gaoli on Weibo, a Chinese social media account. This led to her sudden disappearance and blocking of all her social media accounts. There was even a farcical interview she gave after a month of disappearance where she retracted her statements thus enhancing the needle of suspicion. While the Women's Tennis Association (WTA) took a tough stand not to hold any events in that country despite the massive sponsorship losses, the rest of the sporting world, chiefly the IOC and ATP, either stood silent or made feeble noises so as not to upset the dragon. The boycott of the Beijing Winter Olympics by some countries such as US and Britain would surely have been influenced by this although their official version is about the maltreatment of the Uyghur's by the communist state. This move takes us back to the 1980 and 1984 boycotts of the greatest sporting show on the planet. Is it right to mix sports and politics? On paper, it might seem that it is incorrect but then sport is no longer an amateur pastime bringing people together. It's run along corporate lines and involves a lot of money. No wonder then that so many non-sporting professionals are running federations around the world. Hence, one can never keep politics and sports in its current avatar away from each other. Therefore, boycotts hurt revenues apart from the image and that in itself becomes a potent tool. No wonder that even big ticket leagues such as Indian Premier League (IPL) use politics to keep out foreign players from certain countries. However, what the WTA has done is commendable under the present circumstances. It is important to send the right message to countries like China to respect the right of freedom of speech.

The entertainment industry has also not been left untouched. There seems to be a feeling in the Politburo that no one, even after becoming a global celebrity, can overgrow one's shoe and question systems. It could probably be considered as a threat or a potential threat to the hegemony of the Party. The case in point is that of Zhao Wei, the Chinese actress who suddenly disappeared from the limelight. She was multi-talented, being a singer, director and a corporate leader. The rationale given was that she was cheating on taxes and money laundering. Other cases in point were the arrest of Kris Wu, an actor and singer in August 2021 on charges of sexual assault and the fining of actress Zheng Shuang over tax evasion. Given their credibility, hardly anyone outside China really believes the powers that be in the country.

On the corporate front, no one has been more iconic that Alibaba founder Jack Ma. He has been for many the face of the changing China. Beginning with an online store in his apartment, his firm grew to be one of the largest technology conglomerates that straddled the globe. However, for the authorities, he crossed the Rubicon when he criticized the Chinese financial system on the eve of launching an initial public offering (IPO) in October, 2020. Not surprisingly, he disappeared for a good three months before resurfacing in late January. The video appearances of Ma at a number of places including a rural school in China with a message to dedicate his life to education and public welfare; and an outing on a Hainan golf course only raises suspicion on his whereabouts. There is no doubt that a person as flamboyant as Ma, not being the limelight for so long is strange with possibilities ranging from house arrest to takeover of his empire by government regulators. As part of this swoop, the authorities have also targeted other large corporates like Tencent and Baidu. The strategy has been to nip things in the bud before they can surface and create trouble.

On the literary front, many dissidents such as Ma Jian have highlighted the repression in China with book on Tibet as well as the 1989 Tiananmen uprising. They have become persona non gratia in their country and have to operate from other countries.

Even in the context of their dealing with neighbours, the bullying tactics has been the main weapon. The relationship with India is a point in case. After independence, the Indian government maintained close relations with China which had also come out of colonial rule and established a communist regime. However, the Chinese wanted to keep the embers of the border dispute alive but did not openly talk about it. However, their capture of Tibet and the refuge given to Dalai Lama by India proved to be the turning point. It led to the communist party rabble rousing and eyeing India as a threat to its control over Tibet. It began bullying India and then the border skirmishes led to a full-fledged war in 1962 which India lost on both the eastern and western fronts. It again used the tactics in Sikkim in 1967 but India was prepared this time and managed to defend well. Similar incidents have occurred with most of its neighbours including in the South China sea where they have used the bullying tactics coupled with show of military strength.

The Chinese have also been accused of interfering in democratic elections since it provides them a tool to install favourable regime, if not prevent a China hawk from coming to power. The US Presidential elections of 2020 is a case in point wherein they were accused of cyberattacks and social media posts. They have repeatedly interfered in the Taiwanese elections by brute show of military force.

They have also actively played a part in fostering internal dissensions in many countries. Some of these include the support in terms of weapons and money for Maoists and insurgents in North East part of India as well as supplies to rebels such as the Arakan army fighting the Myanmar government. They have also been subtly and indirectly arming Pakistan for keeping the pressure on India in the Kashmir front.

On the information technology side, they have developed a robust network of hackers who carry out cyberattacks on government sites throughout the world. It provides them with a high level of intelligence and ability to influence a lot of global decisions.

CHAPTER SIXTEEN

Modern China

Despite all the troublesome tactics of China, one must give credit to the economic development of the country which has placed it at the second global rank in terms of GDP. Smart policies have ensured that the economy weathered the storms emanating from the disastrous Cultural revolution. The credit must go to the liberalization which began in 1978 under Deng Xiaoping.

The economic liberalization was more pragmatic and in two stages, the first of which was gradual reforms to unshackle the agricultural sector while maintaining a significant presence of the state owned enterprises in the industrial arena. The student uprising that led to the Tiananmen square crackdown in 1989 led to an hiatus in these reforms.

However, in the second phase, private enterprises were encouraged as the economy liberalized further. These steady reforms ensured that China did not meet the fate of perestroika in the Soviet Union that saw the collapse of the latter. One must also give credit to the Special Economic Zones, largely port based, which gave a fillip to export orientation of the economy that saw huge investments come in. China's red carpet welcome to foreign investment was what saw its economy boom and catch up with the leaders of the economic pack in the western world.

Even in the annexed territory of Tibet, they have created infrastructure in hostile terrain and adverse weather conditions. However, it is debatable as to the benefits of these projects for the indigenous Tibetans. Quite akin to the imbalanced and lopsided development done during the colonial era. The BRI also saw huge infrastructure that was developed for better connectivity.

As one visits the cities of China or undertakes train journeys along the major arteries, there is a sense of awe on the planning and infrastructure created. Even the rural areas alongside the rail tracks give an impression of a developed economy. Some places like the waterfront in Shanghai and the central business districts of the major cities would well be mistaken to be that in the western world. Some of the foreigners who have undergone medical treatment in the country also swear on the standard of medical services there. However, the interiors of the country have still not developed to the same extent. Nevertheless, the country can claim to have elevated a significant percentage of its population above the poverty line.

However, amidst all this overt development, one can sense a strange sense of discomfort as one travels around. The sense of openness among the people is strangely missing and elements of a socialist society that has been under strict surveillance props up at some place or the other. Those who have lived in democratic societies with freedom of speech can sometimes get spooked. One gets the feeling that the people are not able to express their feelings openly and are suspicious towards strangers, mainly foreigners. Without taking names, one incident that has been verified independently from the persons who were at the receiving end of it, needs to be narrated. In a tier 2 city of the country, as some senior government officials of a developing country were travelling by a taxi, they were engaging in some light banter. When the taxi reached its destination, the driver pressed a wrong button and behold, the conversation of the officials which was taped all along the journey, suddenly started to play. The driver fumbled and managed to shut the audio tape. The officials were in a state of shock and one can swear that they kept their mouths sealed in public places from that point onwards till they left the shores of China. It came to light that these drivers were instructed to tape the conversations, specifically of foreigners and are believed to be paid by the state. The big brother watching you syndrome is something that cannot be erased from the societal DNA.

CHAPTER SEVENTEEN

China's Lebensraum Strategy

There is no doubt that when one looks at China's smart strategy for land grabbing, a lot of thought process has gone into it. There is an indeed a method to their madness.

Firstly, it has been the assimilation of the global experience on this, specially the two World Wars. When Germany went into this expansionism, the thought process, which was transparent, was on the basis of racial profiling which was openly advocated by the Reich. This created a global outcry and virtually isolated them. The Chinese however, never used this theory to propound their expansionism. They were just harping on the historical dynasties, chiefly the Qings who had annexed these territories as the main reason behind their claim. However, it is well known that they actually implemented the Nazi theory of claiming these lands for settlements by ensuring that the Han Chinese actually habited these captured lands. It also provided them a leeway to control any dissent by changing the demographic profile of the region. They also did not commit the mistake of signaling out a particular community for genocide as the Nazis did and paid a heavy price. Even in the case of the Ugyhur's, which the communist party believed could be potential threats to their hegemony, internment camps were designed with a view to indoctrinating them. There can be no doubt that these camps would also be grounds for clinical research on neural science advancements for controlling one's mind.

Secondly, religion was one area where the Chinese were smart enough to tread with caution. Being the atheistic state that they were, things were made easier since they did not have or recognized any religion. However, during Mao's Cultural Revolution from 1966-76, religion also became a target with religious freedom severely curtailed in the name of purging all capitalist ideals. Subsequently, the country took a more reformist path. While officially religion is banned, the authorities have allowed people of faiths such as Confucionism, Buddhism etc to worship provided the gatherings were not large and did not pose a threat to the Party's power. Hence, there was always a Damocles sword but religious freedom was not suppressed. However, in the case of captured territories, they had to be more careful. In the case of Tibet, the four Buddhist schools were handled with care. While the Tibetan uprising of 1959 and the Cultural Revolution did lead to the destruction of the monasteries, the phase after the 1980s saw a tempering of this phenomena. Nevertheless, there were real challenges for the religion to survive in communist China.

In Xinjiang, the situation was really precarious with the great distrust the regime had of the Ugyhur's, specifically with reference to potential terror threats. In a set of leaked papers, the thinking of the Chinese regime, perturbed by the 9/11 terror attacks in the US and the London subway bombing, decided to adopt a harsh, no mercy policy, premised on educational remolding of those who were engaging in such activities. Obviously, the fuming Chinese, denied the existence of these papers, but the US experts have painted this policy with many brushes with terms like human rights violation, ethnic cleansing, cultural genocide etc. What is stark is that even today in Xinjiang, religious prayers are to be conducted only inside the house with all the public places like mosques barred from the same. The religious symbols like the skull cap and beard are barred which seems to be a big affront to religious freedom. On the other hand, the re-education centres which China has opened, meant to curtail terrorism, have targeted religion itself, thereby indirectly attributing a causal link. It is believed that more than a million Ugyhur's are interned in these camps.

Thirdly, changing the demographic profile of the annexed territories has been a tactic used by the Communist Party. Without directly saying so, there is an implicit understanding in the Communist Party that the Han Chinese are racially superior to the other denizens of the annexed territories. It is with this view that they were settled in both Tibet an Xinjiang with a view to changing the demographic profile and making the Tibetans and Ughyur's minority in their own land. It would also give a lever to the authorities to manage law and order issues.

Fourthly, the tactics that we China using is that of being opportunistic in land grabbing. Xinjiang was annexed in close cooperation with Russia who had an interest in settling the borders of the Central Asian Republics which were still part of the Soviet Union. In the case of Tibet, with Europe including Russia recovering from the devastating effects of World War and perceiving no threat from India or Nepal which had borders with Tibet, they attacked with a full force from Chomdo coming to the outskirts of Lhasa. With the Americans only providing little support to the Tibetan resistance and Russia keeping its hands off, they launched the full scale attack on the rest of Tibet. As far as India was concerned, they used the period of the Cuban missile crisis when both the Soviet Union and US were busy elsewhere to carry out a two pronged attack on India in 1962. The timing was perfect and India was completely unprepared militarily assuming that its bonhomie with China would tilt the scale in favour of a peaceful negotiation. The South China sea had seen the classic nibbling strategy with show of naval force to subdue the other countries. A similar tactic is being used for Taiwan with a clear intent to conquer the island. It is only the presence of US naval fleet in these contested waters that has made China cringe and not engage in a full scale war. Moreover, as discussed earlier, Russia's plans to invade Ukraine could be the opportunity that is presented on a platter to the communist regime to satiate its nefarious designs on the island. Only time will tell if the show of strength by the US and some other allies through their naval exercises would have any telling effect.

Fifthly, one has to admit that China's strategy is about a shrewd planning. They have created the Belt and Road Initiative (BRI) to economically engage all their neighbours in big projects that would be a counterweight to the west. It is a smart diplomatic move to get these countries on their side and provide China logistics connectivity, both for trade and for military deployments. There is no doubt that China has delivered on the ground in terms of creating this infrastructure in a record time. Even in the occupied territories of Tibet and Xinjiang, they have created massive infrastructure in fairly hostile conditions. This would definitely change the economic face of the region but all this would come at a human cost, i.e. the marginalisation of the indigenous communities including through human right abuses.

Finally, China has also been involved in the tactics of assuming a global power and using unconventional weapons in the process. With the funds at its disposal, it has managed to enter and influence many international organisations. A permanent Membership of the UN provides it enough clout to veto any adverse move. It has also entered into organisations such as the Arctic Council which is considered important for minerals, fauna and navigation in the future. It has smartly allied itself with Russia on critical matters despite not always seeing eye to eye with the former communist country. Militarily, it has built up a potent arsenal, even carrying out nuclear tests in Xinjiang. With little respect for intellectual property, it has reverse engineered many of the western technologies to stay abreast of the latest developments. It has used the dictatorial North Korean regime as a tool to keep the tensions high in the region, thereby maintaining its influence.

Moreover, it may have used biological warfare with the COVID virus having spread from a lab in Wuhan. Howsoever they may deny the latter, the finger of suspicion points to them since they have not cooperated in any WHO investigation on the origins of the virus and have been very guarded on the extent to which the virus has affected them. Many have argued that WHO, to which they provide sizeable funds, has also been severely influenced by them and they can literally ask the organization to parrot their views.

CHAPTER EIGHTEEN

How to counter Sinosraum

China may have achieved most of its objectives under Sinosraum as it has annexed a lot of territories and changed their demographic profile, built up a formidable arsenal of weapons which can challenge even the US and undertaken infrastructure projects such as BRI thereby managing to have a global economic clout.

However, its agenda is still unfinished, the biggest of which is of course the annexation of Taiwan. The other countries would need to understand this reality and unite to stop any such efforts. It is not going to be easy given China's naval power and its aim at ensuring that it controls the navigational routes of the South China Sea. The formation of the QUAD between Australia, India, Japan and US to keep the Indo-Pacific open is probably the first of these steps but other countries are reluctant to join at this point of time. Even Europe, barring a few countries like UK do not want to openly take on the dragon. But eventually they would all realize the futility of being a bystander. It has been this indifference of Europe, albeit after the devastating effects of the WW II, that was responsible for what happened after the communists took over and annexed both Xinjiang and Tibet. How to counter Sinosraum

As for potential hotspots elsewhere like the Indian and Central Asian borders, a firm message has to go to China to try to respect the territorial integrity of the region. The chipping and nibbling strategy has to be nipped in the bud through a more collaborative move.

It is important to raise the ante on China's human rights record. Xinjiang has been at the epicenter of one of the world's worst human right abuses with the Ugyhur's even denied the right to profess their religion including the customs associated thereof. The re-education camps have virtually robbed people of individual rights and liberty. Some figures, point to around a million Ughyur's incarcerated in these camps and held under strict vigil. The situation in Tibet is also precarious with the Tibetans having been marginalized. Hong Kong has come in for a lot of repression as the voice of pro-democracy has been muffled by a pro-Beijing government. The disappearance of Chinese celebrities is another matter of concern and only shows how brutal the regime can be. One may argue whether the boycott of the Beijing Winter Olympics of 2022 is a good move. However, in the circumstances, there was no other option than to place the human rights issue at a global pedestal. Moreover, just like the Tokyo summer games where Russia was not allowed to participate but their athletes did, a similar situation would develop where the athletes can still participate but not under their country's flag.

China would continue to expand its economic clout through BRI as well as large investments in many parts of the world like Africa. It would be foolhardy to really try to stop these projects without making the host country aware of the consequences of their deal with China. While logistics connectivity is an important part of economic growth and enhancement of trade, it is important that one moves away from the model of neo-colonialism that China is trying to impose. The rest of the world can therefore only look at educating the host country and allow them to tap alternate sources of investment. China's role in global growth would be important and the aim is not to look away from China but ensure that any collaboration on the basis of shared partnerships are mutually beneficial.

The post COVID logistics nightmare that was created due to the non-availability of containers and skyrocketing shipping freight costs has also been attributed by some to China. This is on account of the significant share of the country in the global production of containers and in the ownership of the shipping lines. The disruption to trade could also be a mechanism for annulling the anti-China sentiment in the post pandemic environment wherein a lot of buyers were looking at alternate source of supply.

The only hope is that the situation does not deteriorate for the worse as anti-China sentiment after COVID is already at an all-time high. The world seems more mature than in the 1940s. However, the rest of the world has to become more aware of China's pernicious strategy and will surely not turn a blind eye, as it happened during the growth of the 3rd Reich in Germany. The Chinese party would always look for weaknesses to stretch their Lebensraum since they believe that they are at the centre of the world and have the right to rule it. Each and every move would need to be countered effectively with a global collaborative strategy.

Summarising the possible global strategy to counter China's expanstionist policy, one must look at the following:

- Have a global co-ordination to ensure that no more territories are annexed. Taiwan looks to be the next big hotspot followed by the South China sea and India. The world has to be guarded on the Ukrainian crisis being used as an opportunity to invade Taiwan.

- Raise their abysmal human rights records in Tibet, Xinjiang across all international forums and put diplomatic pressure for them to mend their ways.

- Keep the global navigations routes such as South China sea open and any threat from Chinese vessels should be well responded to.

- Use an effective global strategy to tackle possibilities of cyberattacks and unconventional means of warfare like biological from China.

-

Explore measures to take diversify global supply chains rather than concentrating them in particular geographies like China. For this creating domestic production capacities across the globe is crucial and hence credible suppliers need to be identified across the globe.

• International logistics also needs diversification so that the spike in shipping rates and availability of containers for trade are eased. There needs to be a global forum to discuss this.

• The influence of China on international organisations like UN, WHO etc needs to be reduced through diplomatic moves by the other nations. This is crucial to limit China's pernicious intent in buying support of other nations through their financial strength.

References

1.

Open internet sources like Wikipedia

2.

Dr Rajasimman Sundaram: The Relevance of Geography and History in the Maritime Domain: The Indian Defence Review Issue Vol. 34.3 Jul-Sep 2019 Date : 06 Oct , 2019

3.

Dr Abrahamsson: On the Genealogy of Lebensraum: Geographica Helvetia 2013

4.

Roza Nurgozhayeva: How is China's Belt and Road Changing Central Asia: The Diplomat: 9 July, 2020

5.

Major General PJS Sandhu 1962 – Battle of Se-La and Bomdi-La(A View From the Other Side of the Hill and a Comparison with the Battle of Chosin Reservoir)*